Helpless & Hopeless

The Story of Sweatshirt of Hope

Terry Derstine

Dedication

This book is dedicated to my wife of 54 years, and the persons who walked with us and beside us:

Your prayers, faithfulness, and support gave us the courage to tackle another day!

This verse was given by a friend early on in our journey.

Those who have HOPE in the Lord

Will renew their strength.

They will soar on wings like eagles;

They will run and not grow weary,

They will walk and not be faint.

Isaiah 40:31

Written by Terry S Derstine, 2022. All rights reserved

Book editing and project management: Morgan Simpson

Photo Credits

Front Cover: Stoltzfus Photography

Back Cover: Jaselyn Ramos

Acknowledgment

I want to start by thanking our friends, church family, and employees who supported us by listening to our cry for help in a dark time of uncertainty and loneliness. Thank you for supporting us when we felt like giving up and crawling into a hole or running away from our situation.

I want to thank my Lord and Savior Jesus Christ most of all for the scriptures that spoke to me in special moments and were given in His timing. Praising God through Christian radio, hymns, and worship songs carried me through many challenging days. God's hand was evident time and time again as we traveled this road of life.

I would also like to thank the hundreds or even thousands of people across the United States and around the world who prayed for us and our family while feeling helpless and hopeless, not knowing how to take the next step or if we would survive another day.

1 Corinthians 12:12 NIV

"Just as a body, though one, has many parts, but all its many parts form one body, so it is with Christ."

Contents

Dedication	3
Acknowledgment	4
Introduction	7
Chapter 1: God's Call, a Reality	9
Chapter 2: A Life in Uncharted Waters	11
Chapter 3: Broken and Distracted	15
Chapter 4: Life Out of Control	19
Chapter 5: Lord, What Next?	27
Chapter 6: Then Came the Holidays	33
Chapter 7: God's Call	37
Chapter 8: Why A Sweatshirt?	43
Chapter 9: God Calls Again	47
Chapter 10: The Joy of Serving	55
Chapter 11: Journey with Purpose	59
Chapter 12: Unity	63

Introduction

My wife and I grew up in middle-class Christian homes in Souderton, Pennsylvania attending 12 years of school together. A year or so out of high school we started to date and were married 9 months later. Life was off to a great start and several years later we had our first child, a son, and, two years later, a daughter. Life was good, and we felt blessed as a family, only dealing with the normal challenges of life.

However, life changed in 1987 when our daughter turned 15 years old and started to struggle with migraines. The migraines became more intense as time passed, so we kept seeing doctors who did their best to find a cause with no relief or diagnosis. She started missing school and making some poor life choices.

Our daughter grew up attending church, was involved in our youth group, attended a Christian school, and had a solid foundation. She was caring and always helped others as far back as elementary school. She helped the kids who came from broken homes and wanted to give them something so they could feel better.

As life went on our son would tell us things that our daughter was doing, but, being naïve, things did not make sense to us. We were sure this was a sibling rivalry and could not verify some of the things we were told. As a parent, we should have checked into various situations more and believed our son, but we brushed things off too often. We are sorry for the situation and admit this was a mistake on our part as parents, but we cannot go back and fix it. All we can do is ask for forgiveness.

We continued to take our daughter to doctors and emergency room visits; all they would do was prescribe oxycodone time after time.

At the age of 17, the summer before her senior year, our daughter had a traumatic experience that changed the way she handled life. We had no idea anything happened until we received a threatening phone call in the middle of the night. At that point, our daughter moved out of our house and in with our church youth leaders for a month or so. After that time, she came home, shared several words on a piece of paper about what happened, and life went on. No one wanted to deal with the painful situation. Around six months before her graduation, our daughter made another poor choice by dropping out of school and running away to Florida for several months with three friends. She returned from Florida still dealing with migraines, going to the hospital regularly all while attempting to hold a job. At this point she was living in our home, not taking responsibility, and staying out later and later which was really trying my patience. Many times, I felt like this was pushing me to my limits. I would be going to work around 5 a.m., and she was coming home. Something had to change!

Chapter 1
God's Call, a Reality

It was Saturday, September 17th, 2022, and the morning sun was starting to come up over the snow-white tent that had been erected earlier in the week. As we prayed for the day, the presence of God was evident. The countless hours of planning and hundreds of hours of volunteer help were now a reality. Our 1000-seat tent, extensive lighting, and a mountain of sound system equipment now seemed ready for day two of HOPE 22. The beauty of the day along with the building excitement was hard to put into words. Last evening, we came together as a community. We served food, had great fellowship, heard personal testimonies, and were blessed to have the award-winning singers, the 3 Heath Brothers. The night ended with evangelist, Christopher Boyce, sharing the message of **hope** found in Jesus. As we stood in amazement, we were now ready to kick off the morning with our St Luke's University Health | Penn Foundation "Recovery is for Everyone" walk. 200+ walkers bringing awareness to mental health and addiction which is a challenge in our communities.

After the walk, "It is Written" Teen Challenge band will kick off HOPE 22, an all-FREE event with a kids' block party, 57 non-profit organizations offering resources for life's struggles, food trucks, fresh-made donuts, ice cream, musicians, and many personal testimonies. That evening, we were blessed to have Nashville recording artist, Leanna Crawford, with evangelist, Christopher Boyce, share a message of **hope**. The next morning, we were set to finish out with a service hosted by Christian Street Missions. The highlight for many of us was watching nine people being baptized! All for God's Glory! How can we thank enough the 156+ volunteers, many business sponsors, 5 local police departments, fire police, 2 fire companies, 2 ambulance services, and North Penn Goodwill?

As I stood there, in awe of what was happening just off County Line Road in my hometown, the memories of God's vision that was given to me for this and my backstory to all of it come rushing back into my head.

Chapter 2
A Life in Uncharted Waters

Migraines continued, so our daughter was admitted to a hospital in Philadelphia for a week that specialized in migraines. After many tests, changes in diet, brain scans, etc. we heard the words "We do not know how to help your daughter." She was depressed and really struggled with how to live without pain.

She continued to see doctors, and, many times, I would drive her to the emergency room at all hours of the night because of the severity of the migraines. Back in the 90s, it was common to hear doctors say "No one should suffer from pain." They would then prescribe more oxycodone without taking the time to interview our daughter. Late one evening, I questioned a head ER nurse, whom I personally knew, and asked why doctors would give our daughter the meds she requested. The answer was that the doctor had worked a very long shift and wanted to go home. I was upset!

Our daughter started staying out later and later running with the wrong crowd.

1991 – 1992

At the age of 20, our daughter told us that she was pregnant, out of wedlock, and had no father involved. This was a very challenging time as we traveled a road without a clear roadmap. Our daughter was going to have a baby without a steady job, daily migraines, and a guy that was out of the picture. We did hear some criticism from some people that we should have done a better job raising our daughter, but overall, we had support from friends, family, and our church family as we dealt with our situation. People left encouraging notes in our church mailbox. We received letters and cards in the mail, and another gal had a baby shower for our daughter. The encouragement from everyone helped us in these difficult times.

We had some individuals, that struggled in their past, share heartbreaking stories. Everyone was doing their best to encourage us not to give up on our daughter and support her in her time of need.

1992

Our daughter had a beautiful daughter, and we thought things would get better now that she was a mom. However, our daughter continued to struggle.

We were amazed, that in the depth of pain and struggle God kept showing up in miraculous ways time after time.

God was good, but I still struggled with our daughter having a child out of wedlock. One day at work, when I was really struggling, one of my employees, who I was not sure where she was in her walk with the Lord, said "Remember this child is a Gift from God!" WOW! That statement hit me between the eyes. God blessed us with a beautiful healthy granddaughter no matter what our circumstances.

We had close friends who did not judge us and supported us in so many ways even though these times were trying, and we believed this was not God's design for having a child. God was good even in the struggles of life. We never thought we would be in this position, but God humbled us and brought us to our knees time and time again. We kept asking where we went wrong raising our daughter.

Proverbs 22:6 KJV

⁶ Train up a child in the way he should go: and when he is old, he will not depart from it.

As parents, we did our best to keep our sanity in our home, but many times that wasn't enough. Our journey was humbling as we struggled with life not knowing how to manage our family drama.

As parents, we felt helpless and hopeless because we could not fix our daughter's migraines. After years of visiting doctors and hospitals and thousands upon thousands of dollars, we started to become alarmed at the number of prescription drugs issued for reoccurring migraines. She would lay in bed crying with her head covered with a pillow, so she could not see any light. This was a vicious cycle of rebound migraines.

A highlight in the midst of the trials was when our daughter decided to make a commitment to follow Jesus and was baptized. What a glorious day!

Our journey of hurt and concern continued month after month. We told our daughter if she continued to use prescription drugs, she will become addicted. Her response was "I cannot deal with the pain of debilitating migraines. What do you want me to do?"

The migraines intensified, so more drugs were prescribed to maintain a lifestyle of existence. Our daughter was not working a job, and she started staying out later at night, making our life more difficult. My wife had to step in often to take care of our daughter's baby who would be upstairs in her room crying with no one to take care of her.

I came home from work and my wife was taking care of our granddaughter and dealing with our daughter's disrespectful attitude and unwillingness to help around the house. My wife wanted to ask our daughter to leave, but I had a hard time kicking her out of our house with a baby and no money. My wife respected me despite her frustrations from daily challenges. I went to work each day burying myself in the management of our business in order to forget the pain of what was happening at home. These on-going challenges strained our marriage in many ways. We were always on edge.

Chapter 3
Broken and Distracted

We realized that our 22 year old daughter was addicted to opioids.

1994-95

I will never forget our first visit to Penn Foundation Recovery Center. We met with two seasoned addiction counselors. My wife and I, along with a friend from church who came as support, were there to try and figure out a plan. I made the statement that our daughter just "needs to quit". The counselor who was sitting on the other side of the table got up from his chair, got in my face, and said "You do not understand, you just don't quit using drugs. Drugs are powerful, they change your mind and body, they change the way you think and act, and drugs destroy the way you do life. All the person caught up in the cycle of addiction wants to do is get their next fix and they will do anything to get money to buy more drugs. If it means stealing from her own baby's piggy bank, her parents, from their place of employment, or from a neighbor next door, she will steal even if it means you will go to jail. Nothing matters at this point in life."

That was hard to hear, eye-opening, and the truth, but very hard to process not understanding addiction.

My wife and I felt pain, shame, and guilt because of our situation. We didn't know how to help our child. We wanted to run away rather than deal with our child's destructive behavior. We would go to work, community events, and church trying to put on a happy face. When people would ask how we are doing, we would smile and say fine. We suffered silently for a number of years. Inside we were crying out to God for help; we were too proud to be honest with friends, our church, and our community. Every other person we knew had the perfect family, and life was good for them. Our family was falling apart. Life was a disaster from family to closing our business, laying off 55 employees, and being in major debt. We were in a very dark and lonely place.

1994

At this point we had been meeting with Penn Foundation Recovery counselors on a monthly basis, always taking along one of three people from our church for support. They heard things we did not always hear or want to hear. This went on for a long time, and, finally, our counselor asked us to make a very tough decision.

We were encouraged by our counselors to do "tough love". As husband and wife, we could not agree on how to do tough love for a period of approximately 10 months. What if we kicked our daughter out of our home and she had no place to live? How would she get money? What if something would happen to her? What if she did not have money for food? There were so many "what if's" that it was difficult to decide.

If you ever asked your child to leave your home and her baby would remain with you as grandparents, you understand the hurt and agony, the sleepless nights, and days you go to work in a daze with no ability to perform your job. I was not sure how to pray or at this point was not able to pray. I was broken!

We had to do something because our daughter was not taking responsibility for her daughter or working a job. At this point, our counselor recommended we give her a six-month notice to get her act together, or she would need to move out of our house. Our counselor said she knows where the shelters are, so she will have a place to go. With a month to go, we told her the day she had to be out of the house, and we would change all the locks on our doors.

My wife and I needed to get away so we explained we would be taking her child, our granddaughter on vacation with us to Florida and staying with friends. She was fine with us taking her daughter, so she signed a paper saying we had the right to take our granddaughter across state lines and gave her consent in case of a medical emergency. The day came for us to leave, so we had a locksmith change all the locks on all the doors in our house. Our daughter was going to stay at her boyfriend's house, so we left.

1995

This was one of the most difficult times of our lives. We were devastated and felt we failed as parents. Our daughter was 23 years old and addicted to prescription pills. Doctors kept prescribing opioids like they were candy. She was a regular at our local hospital ER and visited local doctors for prescription pills.

Our daughter moved in with a boyfriend about 40 minutes from our house and life went on. We ended up raising our granddaughter because our daughter had no desire to take care of her. Our daughter struggled to keep a job due to doctor's visits, multiple trips on a weekly basis to emergency rooms, hospital stays, along with being on so many prescription pills. Our relationship was like a roller coaster as we dealt with the pain of a daughter who was struggling and as grandparents raising our granddaughter who needed her mom. It was heartbreaking!

Months later our daughter decided she needed help and was ready to go address her addiction. I drove her to Penn Foundation Recovery Center where she met with an awesome in-take counselor to figure out where there was an open bed. We spent six or seven hours in the waiting room as he made call after call in search of an available bed. We finally had an answer that there was a bed available in Malvern. This was a relief, but by this point, we were both on edge because our daughter had not had access to any drugs.

So, we left Penn Foundation on a 45-minute drive to a Pottstown office for processing, and then they would transport our daughter to the Malvern rehab center. At this point, she was detoxing from not using drugs for several hours. She was not able to sit still on the seat, bouncing back and forth the duration of the drive, and sweating profusely. She was very agitated and nervous not sure of what she is getting herself into because this was her first stay at a rehab facility. I am sure it was very scary!

I left the processing office totally exhausted with a million emotions going through my head. I was angry, frustrated, hurt, and felt like a complete failure as a parent. I prayed over and over that this rehab and recovery program would be the answer we had been praying for.

Chapter 4
Life Out of Control

Our daughter's drug use escalated going in and out of many rehab facilities across the country and most times not finishing her 30 days program.

2001

Six years later, while I was traveling to a business trade show in Orlando, Florida, I received a call from my wife saying our daughter was in jail. At 29 years old, she was struggling with migraines and going to hospitals 4 to 5 times a week for drugs. She decided to leave the fellow she was living with and stole his aunt's credit card. She attempted to take cash from the card at Western Union and ended up in jail for theft. My wife said there is nothing I can do and told me to keep going to my trade show, which I did. It was a stressful trip. My wife and the ex-boyfriend went to her court sentencing and saw her from jail on video.

I drove for hours with tears running down my face praying and listening to several gospel CDs by the Gospel Express Prison Ministry Team. Songs they sang in prisons called "Behind the Fences". These songs included "This Is the Day", "Jesus Is Coming Soon", "Because He Loved Me", "But For The Blood", "Praise God He Saved My Soul", "Yes I Know", "Jesus Opened Up The Way",

"When I Get Carried Away", "It's Still The Blood", "That's Reason Enough", "Thank You", "Mama", "Paid In Full", "He's The Rock I'm Leaning On" and many more. The words of the songs kept me going when I felt I could not take another step.

I was praying, and asking God for answers. How can we help our daughter to work through the pain of ongoing migraines? What are we to learn from this situation?

At that point, we did not know how to pray but things kept getting worse. Raising our granddaughter, our daughter would stop in periodically to see her daughter and stand in the doorway falling asleep. We would question her why she was so tired. She always said she had not slept much the night before. My wife and I, being naïve, had no idea what was happening. A number of months later, we found out she had been using heroin and was spiraling out of control. She was only 29 years old. A so-called friend told her if she used heroin, she would not have migraines, which is true. For those who do not know, all it takes is one hit of heroin to become addicted. You are hooked! That is how powerful these drugs are. In 2022, heroin is laced with fentanyl which is much more powerful and deadly in many cases.

Some choices can change your life forever! A very high percentage of people in addiction never find recovery from this awful disease. After a time of using heroin, your brain does not receive enough oxygen needed to make rational decisions.

With that said, I do believe God is still in the Miracle business. He is a Waymaker, so we continue to pray for miraculous healing.

No matter how much our daughter messed up, my wife and I will never give up loving her. I keep going back to scripture. Jesus Never Gave Up Loving us! He always loves us no matter what we have done. However, he wants us to come, lay everything at the foot of the cross, and ask for forgiveness.

One morning while meeting with my Higher Calling businessmen's group, my accountability group, a pastor friend read this passage to me in my time of struggle. It is found in Lamentations.

Lamentations 3: 21-33 (NIV)

21 Yet this I call to mind and therefore I have hope:

22 Because of the LORD's great love we are not consumed, for his compassions never fail.

23 They are new every morning; great is your faithfulness.

24 I say to myself, "The LORD is my portion; therefore, I will wait for him."

25 The LORD is good to those whose hope is in him to the one who seeks him;

26 it is good to wait quietly for the salvation of the LORD.

27 It is good for a man to bear the yoke while he is young.

28 Let him sit alone in silence, for the LORD has laid it on him.

29 Let him bury his face in the dust—there may yet be hope.

30 Let him offer his cheek to one who would strike him, and let him be filled with disgrace.

31 For no one is cast off by the Lord forever.

32 Though he brings grief, he will show compassion, so great is his unfailing love.

33 For he does not willingly bring affliction or grief to anyone.

As a parent, we did not have a clue or understood the drug scene. We wanted to believe our child was just having a bad time as she dealt with her migraines. We did not understand the many signs, patterns, or behaviors a person in an addictive state. We did not understand how we were enabling her with all her manipulations.

Almost every time we met with our counselors, they would tell us "you are enabling your daughter." I would say I am just trying to help and support our daughter, and they would come back forcefully and say "No you are enabling her!"

There are several teaching moments when working with a person in active addiction.

Our daughter would ask for money for gas to get to work and, after some back and forth, I would give her $ 10.00 for gas. The counselor would tell me you just bought her drugs. I said no she needed gas to get to work. The counselor would suggest to just go pump the gas in her car. The next time my daughter needed gas I went with her and pumped the gas, and we caused quite the scene. My daughter is screaming at me at WAWA while putting gas in her car. "You do not trust me!" I yelled back "No, I do not trust you. Trust must be earned."

The holidays came and we always wanted to give our daughter gifts because she needed help. We decided not to give her cash so she could not purchase drugs. We thought we were smart and gave her gift cards. We found out weeks later that she sold her gift cards for less than half the value for cash, so she could buy drugs. I can share story after story about how people in addiction will manipulate whatever the situation to get what they want. It is a life many of us will never understand.

I had a non-profit board meeting in Harrisonburg, VA several times a year. I drove to Virginia one Sunday for our Monday board meeting. I decided not to turn my radio on for my roughly four-hour trip. I prayed and kept asking the Lord to give me direction, and wisdom and to show me His will for my life. I tried to process the words failure and success and asked the Lord to bless me and show me His will. I cried out to God and the song I played over and over in my head that really spoke to me was "little is much when God is in it, labor not for wealth or fame but go In Jesus name."

Our struggles were hidden for a long time until one Sunday morning the Lord spoke to my wife and me individually. We would meet people at church and they would ask how we were doing. My response was the same as it always was. "Fine." I came home from church that Sunday morning and told my wife I felt I was living a life of lies and I hated it and myself for it. She had the same thing happen to her the same morning. Our daughter was in an AZ drug rehab that Sunday, and we were telling people we were fine. That Monday morning, we met with our pastor and shared how God convicted us to stop lying to others. The following Sunday the pastor prayed for our daughter who was in drug rehab in AZ and for our family. When the prayer request was mentioned, I wanted to crawl under the bench. I felt like such a failure because we were the first family to admit in front of the church our daughter was a drug addict.

After church 5 different people felt comfortable sharing their hidden struggles and asked us to pray for them.

God opened our eyes to all the hurt in our church which always looked perfect to us.

We all have a story and many times it is not pretty. So many people put on that smile and say our family has it all together, but many times that is not the case. As I look back, God had a plan and a wild ride that I could never have imagined. In the darkness, there were still many blessings!

It is clear to me there is always **hope** no matter how bad things get. We need to keep trusting God in every situation and prayers will be answered in His time. Looking back, we can see the many prayers that were answered even though not the way we wanted. We are praising God that our daughter is still alive after the many,

many times she overdosed, had Hep C, and many drug deals that went bad.

We kept attending regular counseling sessions to help us understand addiction and ways to move forward in the midst of pain. We were so blessed to have faithful friends who went to every meeting with us and walked with us every step of the way. They could hear the things we did not hear or could bare to hear. Over the years our daughter spent time in dozens of rehabs and recovery homes across the US. When she was staying in local facilities, we were able to visit her Sunday afternoons for family time, listening to story after story of families torn apart by addiction. These people were from every walk of life: wealthy business persons, poor persons, men, women, teenagers, moms, dads, doctors, accountants, teachers, white people, people of color, different nationalities. They were people who looked like you and me, the average Joe you would see in your church.

We had many situations that were less than desirable as she moved from place to place, stayed with so-called friends, and some houses for those in recovery until one evening she left one of these recovery houses and went on the run. I received a call from the lady in charge of the house she had been staying at to pick up all the belongings she left behind. I drove an hour on a miserable dark rainy evening to the location, and, when I arrived, the lady in charge took me to a room and told me to pack everything and get it out of there. She was very upset and did not treat me well which made me angry. I was not in a good state of mind at this point. To say I was upset and angry is probably an understatement. We found out later there was a warrant out for her arrest, and she figured the law would not travel halfway across Pennsylvania to arrest her. She stayed in the Altoona area for several months and then ended up in a recovery house in Wilkes Barre, PA. We did go see our daughter in that recovery facility and had a conversation that she should turn herself in to the authorities. Several weeks later she agreed to go to the Northampton County courthouse to turn herself in. A very compassionate, loving lady and her dad from our church drove over an hour to pick up our daughter in Wilkes Barre and drop her off at the Northampton County courthouse. She turned herself in and dealt with the consequences and challenges from that point.

Our daughter moved home again for a period of time which, in hindsight, was not a good move. Life was rocky and always confrontational. Our daughter said she could not deal with her migraines, my harassment, and life in general, so I took her to Grandview Hospital where they checked her out. I was not in the emergency room with her, but the nurse came out and said they felt my daughter was suicidal. They decided to transport her to another facility. They placed her in an ambulance and transported her to a psychiatric hospital in Chestnut Hill, PA. She was admitted for four or five days, and no visitors were allowed. That following Sunday afternoon, one of our pastors and his wife went to the hospital and somehow were able to get her to come to a window on the second floor to talk with her through the bars from outside in the yard.

It seemed like it was one issue after another, but, in the midst of our daughter's struggles, she was always trying to take care of others. She had a heart of gold giving her clothing to someone who did not have anything. If she had any money, she would give her last penny because she would say they needed help more than she did. She would drive people who did not have a car to doctor appointments, hospitals, or a methadone clinic for their daily legal fix. She would call my wife and me and ask if we could help someone in one way or another. Giving to others was an awesome gift, but our daughter was not taking care of herself.

With all the great gifts our daughter had she still struggled to help herself and get out of the muck in her life. I had to take her for random drug testing in Northampton County 40 minutes from our house multiple times a month. One particular time I drove her for her drug test and she gave me a story she was really thirsty drinking a half gallon of ice tea in the span of the drive. After taking her drug test, the woman who administered the test came and told her the test came back inconclusive. It now made sense. She knew her test would come back hot and figured out a way to make her test inconclusive. People in active addiction do their best to outsmart the authorities knowing the outcome of their test.

Chapter 5
Lord, What Next?

2006

While doing drugs and life spiraling out of control there was another pregnancy and a second child creating more heartache and more tough choices. At this point, our recovery counselor advised us to discontinue all contact with our daughter as she continued her unhealthy lifestyle. For the next eight months, we did not have any contact with our daughter. Those eight months were difficult not knowing if she was under doctor's care for this child, dead or alive and if the drug use continued.

I remember the heartbreaking day our daughter texted me asking if she could come home for Christmas. I called our counselor and he said **no**. We were advised not to make any decisions on our own because of the manipulations by our daughter and our emotions taking over. That felt horrible to tell her "You are not able to come home for Christmas." At this point, she had not seen her daughter for eight months as well. We were on an emotional roller coaster with no way to get off.

Four weeks later while sitting at a car wash one Saturday morning, I received a text message from our daughter telling me she was having her baby the following week if I cared. I did not respond to anything without our counselor's support, so I called our counselor. He said to respond and ask if she wanted us there when she delivered her child. I texted her, and she responded asking my wife and I to come a day after the baby was born. At this time, we were not aware this was a very high-risk delivery due to drug use. We were blessed with our fourth grandchild. Our son and his wife blessed us with two grandchildren a number of years prior to this situation.

Fourteen years after her first child was born our daughter had another beautiful daughter, born January 24, 2007. Sadly, she was born addicted at birth. We did go to the hospital to see our new granddaughter on the second day. We had not seen or spoken with our daughter in the last eight months, so we did not know the type of reception we would get. Well, we received a very cold welcome from our daughter and a lady friend who was helping her. We saw our granddaughter laying in her little bed jumping periodically due to her detoxing from her mom's drug use. It was heartbreaking and soon left in tears wondering what was next.

2007

Our daughter moved in with two women for several months who were helping her with her baby. Soon that ended and our daughter decided to go on her own.

At that time our daughter decided to raise her second child on her own in a low-income apartment in Telford half a mile from our house for the next 18 months. This was not an ideal situation, but we were praying it would work out.

We had a key to the apartment and would go there pretty much on a regular basis to help with the baby and our daughter. We were concerned with the lifestyle she was living, but she was an adult. We did not have much of an influence on what she did. Different people came and went from her apartment which raised some red flags but were not able to see anything illegal.

We were sure some drug use continued and knew police came to her apartment and other apartments in the complex various times but never found out the truth. We saw things we did not like but at that point, not many options existed. Turning our daughter into children and youth was not a good option.

2008

When our granddaughter was 18 months old our daughter had to go to court. Her daughter was grabbed by children and youth personnel while our daughter was walking through the halls of Bucks County courthouse and placed in the foster care system in Philadelphia for several months with only the clothes on her back. She did not have her own blanket, any of her own toys, or anything else she was used to having. My wife immediately started making phone calls for hours on end to figure out how to get our granddaughter back and have her placed with some friends. It was a total nightmare. No one wanted to give us any information. Grandparents had no legal rights to this child or basic information back in those days. All we heard from children and youth was that she cried a lot.

Prior to our granddaughter being taken by children and youth, my wife was walking through the hall at church one Sunday and a friend said to my wife "If you ever need a babysitter for your granddaughter, I am available."

To back up a number of years, the woman that said that had attempted to help our daughter with her addiction. Their family took our daughter in when she returned from a short stay in an AZ rehab. Things did not end well with that short-lived experience because she decided not to follow house rules, and, one night while she was out, all her belonging were placed on the porch with no place to go. I received a call from our daughter in the middle of a violent rain and thunderstorm telling me she was homeless. I understood why she was homeless and was furious she would not follow house rules. Prior to this incident, we were told by our counselors to be clear she was not able to return home so I picked her up and dropped her off at a hotel rooming house. I felt terrible dropping her off there, but knew that is what I had to do. I cried buckets of tears all the way home.

When children and youth took our 18-month-old granddaughter from her mom, my wife called our friend and filled her in on our situation and asked her if she and her husband would consider being foster parents. They prayed about the opportunity and said yes, they would take our granddaughter and started the long process to apply to become foster parents.

Finally, after several months of challenges, they were granted foster parent status. For three years our daughter would have supervised visitation with many challenging bumps along the road. Nothing was easy at this point.

After two years in the foster program, our daughter went to children and youth with an accusation of abuse against our granddaughter by the foster dad, a high school principal. We received a call from children and youth asking if we could take care of our granddaughter for a few weeks because she was no longer allowed to stay in the foster home. We asked why and were told nothing. We called the foster family, and they were not able to share anything. We were in the dark, and, several days later, three different case workers came to our house to interrogate us about the foster family for hours. Many times, they were asking the same questions with different twists.

Several weeks later we received a call from children and youth telling us we had to go to Missions Kids in Norristown for questioning regarding the accusation of abuse of our granddaughter. We arrived at Missions Kids and our daughter and a friend were in the waiting room as well. The tension we felt sitting in the same waiting area was unbelievable. My wife and I were filled with anger, hurt, and disappointment as we waited to be interviewed!

Our daughter's friend, who was conspiring with our daughter, went in to be questioned first and came out flustered. Our daughter went in to be interviewed next, and she came out looking flustered and sweating profusely. They left. My wife and I were next and we were both escorted to the interview room together. They asked if we believed the allegation was credible and if there were any indications we saw in our granddaughter now that she lived with us a few weeks that something happened to her. We said we knew without a shadow of a doubt the allegation was false. They explained what happens when the interview is conducted. They have a camera focused on the person's face that is being interviewed so they can see each facial expression and another camera on the person's body, so they can see every reaction and movement. Behind a 2-way window sat a DA, a local investigator, a lawyer, and our local police detective monitoring the person being interviewed. At that point, we were told we would not be interviewed because all indications were this story was fabricated by our daughter and her friend. The foster father still had to go through more interrogation the following week at another location and was then given a clear record.

After several challenging years with the foster care system, and challenges from our daughter, our friends were able to start the adoption process and finalize the adoption of our granddaughter in 2013. The Lord answered our prayers!

We cried out to the Lord… Lord, what are we to be learning on this painful journey? Our daughter has been through the legal system, court appearances, been in jail, lived on the streets of Kensington in Philadelphia in a tent city under the L, lived in a car, floated from house to house, couch surfing, and many rehabs across the country and is still struggling. Addiction ruins families; not just the person struggling. We have not been together as a family for many years. It hurts!

I kept hearing the verse quoted from Romans 8:28

"And we know in all things God works for the good of those who love him, who have been called according to his purpose."

With the promise from scripture that everything works together for good, we were blessed and thankful for the many people who walked with my wife and me over the last 40 years. Our faith is much stronger today because of our journey, our faith, and faithful Godly friends. Yes, we have been harshly judged time after time again for doing a poor job raising our child, and for mismanaging several businesses, but we had many more people step up and support us and tell us God loves us.

Every time we had meetings with our daughter in court, counseling sessions, rehab, recovery houses, and police stations someone from our church family always went with us as a support team. Many times, one of the amazing Penn Foundation counselors would go with us to the Northampton County court sessions as support and tell us what will happen after our daughters' sentencing. He had worked in the system previously and had knowledge of how things worked.

No one will ever know what it meant to my wife and I that some people truly cared. It strengthened our Faith! We were encouraged and given **hope** in the midst of turmoil as people gave hours of their time to support us, pray with us, and walk beside us.

At this, point in 2022, our daughter still struggles and is not involved with us as parents, the daughter we raised, and her 2 children (her granddaughters), or the second daughter that was adopted. Her daughter's adoption was a closed adoption so she is not able to have contact with her unless our daughter gets healthy and then the family will evaluate the situation.

Life has been a roller coaster. As we look back, we are starting to see how God is weaving a pattern of blessings through pain and trials allowing us to trust that everything happens in His timing and for His Honor and Glory.

Chapter 6
Then Came the Holidays

Then came the holidays. Many people do not understand the painful reality of addiction during the holiday season. This is a very difficult time of the year for many. It creates anxiety, stress, and fear of the unknown. Will someone make a scene and get upset over something that really does not matter? Many "what ifs" arise again. We know we need to walk on eggshells or someone will explode and create more drama. Maybe our family members will make the choice not to come to our house this Christmas season.

We have many friends and families who dread the holiday season because of the hurt caused by having a child or family member who struggles with addiction. Our friends' kids are leading worship at church, and our child is in rehab. Our friends' kids are Christmas caroling or attending a fun holiday party, and we wonder if we will get the phone call that our child overdosed and is in the hospital or dead. We live with this every day. We watch other families enjoying their kids and grandkids as a family, but we deal with caseworkers and the foster care system. We get caught up in a helpless, hopeless spiral of our legal system, the manipulation of someone struggling with addiction, lies, attorneys, and the courts. It is a nightmare that seems to never end. We check Facebook on a daily basis to see if our daughter is posting anything and is still alive.

This is where we as parents and siblings have a choice…. to get Better or Bitter. The question I ask myself many times is what does Jesus ask of me?

Scripture clearly states we need to love and forgive those who hurt us.

Mark 11:25

"And when you stand praying, if you hold anything against anyone, forgive him or her, so that your father in heaven may forgive you your sins."

This is easier said than done. I remember the word from several of our recovery counselors. "As long as there is breath there is **hope**. "Do not give up on your daughter. Continue loving your child, forgive them but do not enable them." This is a tall order.

As we try to understand our journey, we continually cry out to God asking how can we face another day and what can we learn through these trials. God has always carried us through trials even though we did not understand. Many times, in our lowest moments, we would get a word of encouragement from someone who years later never remembered saying those words in a time of crisis. We would find a note in the mail or in our church mailbox or get a hug from an unexpected person who said they were praying for us.

Our goal is to find the many blessings we have and not to be overwhelmed with the issues that seem to control our lives. God is good in so many ways. We have been blessed with grandchildren, friends, employees, co-workers, and a Lord and Savior who died for us all. Many times, I think of the song "Day by Day" and with each passing moment, the strength I find to meet my trials here. Trusting in my father's wise bestowment, I've no cause for worry or for fear. When things look bad, remember to trust God and know that God is enough.

While attending a non-profit board meeting years ago, I was given a rock with a verse written on the stone. It was Psalm 62: 5 & 6: "Find rest, O my soul, In God alone; my **hope** comes from him. He alone is my rock and my salvation; he is my fortress; I will not be shaken." This verse says it all and still lies on my desk today.

The reason we share our story is to let people know they do not need to walk this road alone. My wife and I were in denial for many years, unwilling to deal with the truth and no idea where to go for help. There is help available, so reach out to someone you can trust. After over 30 years of questioning God, we realize God allowed us to travel this road of life in order to help others just starting their journey. We accepted God's call to reach out to families whom the Lord lays on our hearts so we can meet, listen to their heartbreaking stories, and say it is ok not to be ok. We always clarify when meeting with others that we do not have answers, but know the pain. We often let families know what steps worked for us and what did not work but each situation is different. We want to encourage anyone if in a similar situation to reach out to someone who has been traveling this road for support and to learn the hard truth about addiction even when it is hard.

My prayer every morning is "Here I am Lord, use me for your honor and Glory."

Chapter 7
God's Call

Yes, a clear call from the Lord!

My question is "Lord, how can I do any more for you?" Our family is falling apart; I am serving at church, on a board, helping with other ministries, and doing my best to manage my own business. "Why me Lord?" There are many other people much more gifted than I will ever be.

I heard the Lord say "When we go through trials, God gives us the opportunity to become that someone for others. "

As we receive God's comfort, we are made better comforters.

In 2 Corinthians 1:4, Paul reminded the Corinthian church that the difficulties they were enduring and the comfort from God they were receiving would enhance their ministry as comforters.

Galatians 6:9

"Let us not become weary in doing good, for at the proper time we will reap a harvest if we do not give up."

2013

God gave me a clear vision on a cold snowy Thanksgiving morning that I need to share the message of **Hope** with those struggling with a program called "Sweatshirt of HOPE." While lying in bed feeling Helpless and Hopeless, all I could invasion was our daughter sitting on the front porch step with her hood up and zoned out. In a matter of one hour, God gave me a vision that He was calling me to encourage those struggling and make a difference in our community. I spent the day praying and putting the vision He gave me onto paper. Then I quickly tried to justify why I could not follow through with these words. I was too busy, and we did not have money. Additionally, I am not an up-front speaker kind of person. So, at that point, I put the document away.

I knew in my heart when God gave me this vision with this clarity, I needed to do something with it even though I did not know the outcome. This was out of my comfort zone, so I filed the document time and time again. However, the Lord kept the vision top of mind until I had to do something.

I was hoping someone would understand my dilemma. After some time, I called my friend John, a radio station manager at 107.5 Alive FM radio, and asked if he had time to meet after he went off the air. He said yes, so I drove over 40 minutes to Boyertown, Pennsylvania, and met John. I explained I had a clear vision from the Lord, but I felt I was not able to follow the call. I gave John the 1-page document with the vision the Lord gave me. He read it and said "What are you going to do with this vision?" I started to justify why I could not answer the Lord's call. He said "You do not have a choice; this is a clear detailed vision God gave you." John prayed with me and for me. I left our meeting and put the paper away once again.

2014

Over the next weeks and months, John gently poked me time and time again. He kept asking "Are you going to answer the call?" I said no, but he did not give up on me. Thankfully, he kept challenging me without badgering me.

So, when someone tells you that God gave them a vision, we need to continue to pray for that person and gently poke them. God used my friend John to challenge me and gave me permission to try to do my best with the gifts I was blessed with. It is not about me, but all about God, trusting Him, being His servant, and mouthpiece to share the "Good News we have been given.

After months of holding back, we created a final logo design and printed 94 sweatshirts hoping John would leave me alone.

The message on the sweatshirt was clear. God Loves You because of the Cross and gives us **HOPE** no matter what our situation. Each sweatshirt has a card in the hoody pocket with the question "If you die today, where will you spend eternity?"

As of 2022, we have distributed over 5,000 HOPE sweatshirts with the encouraging words "HOPE - God Loves You!" God has stretched me more than I could ever have imagined! The Lord provided peace and strength through many valleys and gave me **hope** with many mountaintop experiences. God has been opening doors for me to share my faith journey with other individuals struggling in business, others in the early stages of family addictions, and others struggling with wayward children, health, finances, and mental illness. God opened our eyes and helped us understand that we are not to judge because no one knows what is behind each issue and struggle. We all have a story! I know God has gifted me to be an encourager and not to judge those who are hurting and in pain. I can look back on our journey and see experiences through a different lens than many in our community because of our journey of pain, hurt, disappointments, and struggles. God is good, and He gives us **hope**!

In Isaiah 43:2 we read "When you walk through the fire, you shall not be burned". God does not work in minutes, hours, or days. He works in seasons. The potter knows how long the clay must stay on the wheel to become a thing of value, beauty, and usefulness. We need to trust Him in everything.

Several passages that helped me many times on my faith journey:

II Corinthians 4: 8-9

"We are hard pressed on every side, but not crushed; perplexed, but not in despair; persecuted, but not abandoned; struck down, but not destroyed."

Isaiah 40:31 – Sweatshirt of Hope theme verse

"Those who have HOPE in the Lord will renew their strength. They will soar on wings like eagles; They will run and not grow weary; they will walk and not be faint."

Let us educate each other by talking and listening to stories from those who traveled into these deep valleys but found **hope** on the mountaintop!

"But, not me Lord! I am busy, broken, worn out, and overwhelmed by all of life's struggles. I cannot do anything else!"

A devotional that speaks volumes and encourages me to keep going.

STREAMS IN THE DESERT by L.B. Cowman

"I will make thee a new sharp threshing instrument (Isaiah: 41:15).

A bar of steel worth five dollars, when wrought into horseshoes, is worth ten dollars.

If made into needles, it is worth three hundred and fifty dollars;

if into penknife blades, it is worth thirty-two thousand dollars;

if into springs for watches it is worth two hundred and fifty thousand dollars.

What a drilling the poor bar must undergo to be worth this! But the more it is manipulated, the more it is hammered, and passed through the fire, and beaten and pounded and polished, the greater the value."

May this parable help us to be silent, still, and long-suffering. Those who suffer most are capable of yielding most; and it is through pain that God is getting the most out of us, for His glory and the blessing of others.

Chapter 8
Why A Sweatshirt?

As I meet with various supporters and sponsors many would ask the question "Why a Sweatshirt?" "Are you just handing out sweatshirts? What is the value of the sweatshirt other than a warm garment?"

One of my answers is that this sweatshirt is a ministry vehicle and a tool. Each sweatshirt reminds everyone we have **hope** no matter what we did in the past plus each hoody pocket includes a card asking a very important question. "If you die today, where will you spend eternity?"

Steps are listed on the card to ask Jesus into their heart along with a phone number with a 24/7 prayer hotline for immediate help and support.

Sweatshirt of Hope impacts thousands by sharing the message of **hope** on printed apparel and that God Loves each of us. This message of **hope** opens doors for us to share the gospel. Below is a testimonial, a divine appointment or you can say it is a providential circumstance.

Here is one of many stories regarding the value of a sweatshirt.

A 15-year-old was working in a retail store as a cashier when a middle-aged lady came in looking very sad and saw the HOPE Sweatshirt the cashier was wearing. She said "Your sweatshirt says,

God Loves You!" The lady said "God does not love me. The cashier responded "Yes, He loves you!" the lady said "No He does not love me because of all the bad things I did in my life." The cashier told the lady "We are all broken, but God loves us no matter what we did in our past."

The 15-year-old asked the lady if she could pray with her and for her and the lady said yes and broke down crying. The cashier said she was shaking and prayed with the lady, and, after, the lady raised her hands and said "Thank you God for saving me." The 15-year-old said she could feel the Holy Spirit present at that moment! She said "I am not sure what I prayed, but I know God gave me the words to say."

The cashier told the lady about HOPE 22 and that should attend the event. The lady took a picture of the sweatshirt and said she wanted to attend. She never saw the lady again.

I am praising God for this 15-year-old and her boldness to share the good news of the gospel! May this challenge each of us to share the gospel because we do not know when our time on earth will end.

These stories are not about me or Sweatshirt of Hope, but the witness to God's amazing grace and mercy all for His glory!

When we wear apparel that shines the light of Christ in this dark world, it often starts conversations that would not have happened if we were wearing generic name-brand apparel. So, be committed to wearing apparel that shares the Good News of Jesus.

Here is another story.

A truck driver was parked in an alley early one morning, making a delivery to a farm market, when a lady came out from the building to dispose of her trash. He greeted her and had some general conversation. She asked him about the HOPE T-shirt he was wearing. He shared what Sweatshirt of Hope was and went on to share the gospel her. When people ask, we need to be bold enough to share the gospel. He did not see her again but was faithful by planting seeds from scripture.

1 Corinthians 3:7

"So, neither he who plants nor he who waters is anything, but only God who gives the growth."

Galatians 6:2

"Carry each other's burdens, and in this way, you will fulfill the law of Christ."

Be vulnerable and share your story and journey with others, so, if they are struggling, they feel safe to share. People came to us with their hurt, disappointment, and failures without the fear of judgment because we were willing to share our struggles.

Chapter 9
God Calls Again

One afternoon in 2018, while driving back from a New York City trade show, God gave me another vision. God gave me a clear call to host some type of community event with live music and a safe place for people to go and speak with someone working with a non-profit organization. A place where anyone could ask questions about addiction, eating disorders, and mental illness who were experiencing deep dark valleys in life. I needed a place where anyone searching for how to find victory from oppression and struggles could go. This could be a place our community could get free help and education without feeling judged and learn how social media and TV can lead to destruction.

2018

Here I am processing another clear call and vision from the Lord. I kept hearing the Lord say "What are you willing to risk to help those who are struggling?"

God's call kept getting louder, so I sat down one weekend and created a plan, the vision I felt the Lord gave me. I listed things I felt convicted of that our community needed based on our experiences with our daughter. Many people in our community were not educated on the topics of mental health, addiction, sex trafficking, eating disorders, depression, infertility, and many other topics.

The vision the Lord gave me was to bring our non-profit resources, law enforcement, the business community, and churches together as a team all for His Glory!

I presented my vision to our outreach team at church, which I chaired, and, after some hesitation, someone spoke up and said "This is your vision, you need to run with it. You do not need the church, but I want to make it clear that we will support you in whatever you decide to do."

Matthew 25:35-36 *was a verse that spoke to me.*

For I was hungry and you gave me food,	(God's people are to help those in need)
I was thirsty and you gave me drink,	(God's people are to give Living Water)
I was a stranger and you welcomed me,	(We are to welcome those who are lost)
I was naked and you clothed me,	(We can give you a sweatshirt)
I was sick and you visited me,	(We are to care for those struggling)
I was in prison and you came to me.	(In prison in my own body without Hope)

Here are some thoughts and initial ideas the Lord gave me in a vision.

HOPE FESTIVAL - A Community Event hosted by Sweatshirt of Hope

Our Mission was to be the hands and feet of Christ!

Our Vision was to offer **HOPE** to individuals, parents, grandparents, schools, communities, and churches.

Our Purpose was to provide a safe place offering RESOURCES and contact information to persons feeling helpless and hopeless!

Get Involved by Caring, giving our Heart and Time to our community by sharing God's Love with those who struggle and need **HOPE!**

<u>What I envisioned after I decided to follow God's call was:</u>

<u>An Outdoor Event that Shines the Light of Jesus & Awareness on Issues in our Community!</u>

<u>A goal was to provide information on where to go for help and hear stories from those who struggled and found victory!</u>

My first order of business was to create a team that understood some personal or family dysfunction, pain, and loss, and passionate about sharing God's Love with our community. I met with many people one-on-one from all walks of life and shared the vision the Lord gave me and from there built an amazing team.

Our team included a co-chair who dealt with tragedy in her family, a chief of police who experienced dysfunction in our communities, a radio station manager who received phone calls from listeners in distress, a CPA, business owners, employees, youth leaders, pastors, mom's, dad's, non-profit directors, musician, sales representatives and more.

We spent hours in meetings to create an event that would bring our community together for fun, a time of worship, free food, live music, testimonies from people who came from the pits of hell to find **hope** in Jesus. We wanted to have non-profit organizations offer resources to those struggling in life.

Prior to our event, we hosted an evangelism training seminar led by a young lady from the Fellowship of Christian Athletes to help us understand how and why to share the good news with those whom we would meet. This was an amazing time of equipping God's people to go and share the Good News of Jesus.

Our 1st Annual HOPE Festival was held on September 7, 2019

Time: 10 am to 2 pm. (4-hour event).

Location: on the property of Franconia Mennonite Church

We had approximately 1,000 people attend from 4 states. Four local police departments were involved and the Souderton Ambulance for first aid. We offered free food, live music, 40 non-profit organizations hosting tables with individuals sharing their stories and testimonies, and many volunteers. We heard testimonies from the stage including professional soccer star, Matthew Maher, who shared his story from victory and success to prison and sharing the **hope** we have in Jesus. Matthew Maher is from Coastal Christian in Ocean City, NJ (now Landmark Church) and finished off his message with an alter call.

Then in January 2020 Sweatshirt of Hope held a community pastor's breakfast. Telford Police Chief, Randall Floyd, shared a story about how he had a call while being a detective where a young girl took her life. He arrives at the scene and asked mom "Who can I call that can support you and sit with you?" Her answer was "I Have No One". Heartbreaking! People move because of employment, broken relationships, divorce, and or issues they created in that community. The officer needed to conduct his investigation but was not able to because the mom was hanging onto her daughter. The officer needed help. Detective Floyd called his pastor who was able to come and sit with this mom, pray, and share verses of comfort.

After our breakfast, the Lord gave me the vision to work on the idea to create a faith-based community action team "Linking HOPE 4 LIFE"! We would work to link police, first responders, non-profit organizations, churches, and the business community for just such a situation. Then, when the police have a situation where the persons say they have no one, they are able to reach out to a community action team for support and can complete their investigation.

The vision was "Linking HOPE 4 LIFE" bringing our community together, to understand mental, physical, and spiritual needs and share resources for a healthier community! This program has been not been totally implemented as of 2022 and has undergone several changes as we discussed the possibility.

After the pastor's breakfast, our HOPE Festival team felt the Lord leading us to do a 2nd Annual HOPE Festival on September 17, 2020, during Covid. We prayed, discerned, and ultimately felt the Lord calling us to host the event because so many persons were struggling in isolation. Our team met and discussed issues based on health risks, managing the event with all the CDC guidelines, and so on. We could not all agree but those who were willing to move forward created a plan.

We had one main goal and that was to help and support persons struggling with anxiety, addiction, loss of a loved one due to Covid, and those living in fear. We added a Job Fair, brought back many Non-Profit organizations that offered resources, and partnered with Emmanuel Lutheran Church to distribute boxes of food and meats to families struggling to purchase groceries. 41 Non-Profit Organizations shared resources, along with the job fair, and four local police departments were involved. We offered live music, balloon artists, and face painting, a few people shared personal testimonies, and speaker Matthew Maher shared how he found **hope** in the midst of darkness to approximately 700 attendees.

Our event was held on the property of Franconia Mennonite Church

Time: 10 am to 2 pm. (4-hour event).

It was a very successful event in a time of uncertainty.

One valuable thing the Lord taught our team was to have faith over fear and answer His call for His honor and glory! God's call was clear to host another community event.

3rd Annual HOPE Festival September 16-19, 2021

We expanded to a 4-day and 6-event HOPE Fest in these challenging times as we dealt with Covid and the many issues the pandemic created. Our team felt the Lord's call to expand and move forward because God's plan is greater than ours.

As we discussed plans for HOPE 21, we heard that some community people would not attend an event held on church property, so we started investigating another option. I met with a local landowner who had property a stone's throw from the church and asked if we would be able to set up a large tent on the property. He agreed so we planned HOPE 21 would be held in a cornfield.

To host this event, we set up a 1,000-seat tent along route 113 in Franconia, PA with many local businesses and individuals supporting us. We needed a larger sound system with 3 LED screens, an internet connection for live-streaming our event, special lighting for video production, inside the tent and outside electric and lighting, signage, parking/shuttle buses, port-o-pots, trash dumpster, and so much more. Our amazing community rallied around the idea of sharing the message of **HOPE** in these challenging times. God blessed our team with over 90 volunteers, financial support, and so many others. God is good!

The event planning was going great with me spending hundreds of hours planning HOPE 22 along with our committed team. Then life changed. I ended up with a severe case of Covid, feeling like I may not live and be unable to do anything several weeks prior to the event. I cried out to God pleading to heal me. I wanted to help share the message and "Good News" with our community by showing we cared for them no matter how messed up their lives were, what they did in the past, or what their lives look like right now.

That was not God's plan for me. God sent a group of approximately 10 prayer warriors late one afternoon when I was feeling down and hurting to pray for me. They stood out in the yard so I opened the window and heard these dear brothers and sisters passionately praying for my healing if it was God's will. After the first week, I felt a peace only God could provide that He wanted me to stay home and pray for our team, for the organizations involved, and for our community. I prayed for a community revival!

Thursday night was a red, white, and blue night with a concert presented by the Resilient (wounded warriors) Band. Friday evening's live-in concert was the Alan Scott Band with Alan sharing his struggles with drugs, prison, and a life that was a mess to finding Jesus. Saturday evening Nashville's recording artist, Anne Wilson, shared her struggles with her brother dying in an auto accident at an early age. Her song "Let me tell you about my Jesus" hit the top of the charts a week or so before HOPE 21. Our keynote speaker, Matthew Maher, shared the gospel Thursday and Saturday evening and Sunday morning. Many other people shared their stories from darkness to finding light in Jesus. We hosted a job fair again, with more than 35 non-profit organizations hosting tables along with Emmanuel Lutheran Church distributing food to those struggling for the second year.

God continues to call us to reach out to our community and share the Good News of Jesus we have been given.

Our board felt called to do our 4th outreach event. As we started to plan HOPE 22, we were looking for another location that could have on-site parking. This required a large property. We prayed and the Lord revealed a 23-acre property blocks from my house. I called the property owner and was given approval, and then township approval.

4th Annual HOPE Festival September 16-18, 2022

We stand in amazement at how God's hand was evident as we planned HOPE 22 and the excitement we experienced. What an amazing community outreach!

Chapter 10
The Joy of Serving

After Hope 21, Hope 22, and my challenging Covid experience, I felt God calling me to go into full-time service with Sweatshirt of HOPE. We are not guaranteed another hour or another day, so I need to answer His call now.

I kept saying to the Lord and trying to justify why it was not a good idea for me to be a full-time volunteer for Sweatshirt of Hope. We have very little retirement money set aside, basically living on a fixed income, so wouldn't it be more responsible to take care of my wife and me first? I had many excuses.

God kept calling me and saying I have this. I am enough!

Philippians 4 10 -13

"I rejoice greatly in the Lord that at last, you have renewed your concern for me. Indeed, you have been concerned, but you had no opportunity to show it.

I am not saying this because I am in need, for I have learned to be content whatever the circumstances.

I know what it is to be in need, and I know what it is to have plenty. I have learned the secret of being content in any and every situation, whether well-fed or hungry, whether living in plenty or want.

I can do everything through Him who gives me strength!"

I want to acknowledge our amazing board of directors. Linda, Rita, John, and Mario have the same passion and drive to help those struggling and to share the light of Jesus in this dark world we live in. We are unified when it comes to being good stewards of our finances provided by individuals and business sponsors to print and distribute HOPE-branded apparel and manage costs for our events. It is amazing how God gave each of us different gifts to be used all for His Glory. In unity, we can all say Sweatshirt of Hope is not about us but about Jesus our Lord and Savior. To Him be all honor and glory!

January 31, 2022, I answered the call to be a full-time volunteer for Sweatshirt of Hope working to manage events and meeting with people who were struggling, interested in helping our ministry, and various individuals and business sponsors. Our 501c3 ministry has no paid staff, and we do not accept any government money.

God had a plan! Looking back, I can see how God used others to encourage us when life was a mess. I focused on the suffering of what was missing such as family unity, dysfunction, hurt, and pain but not seeing God's hand weaving patterns of joy and love into our story.

As I reflect back on a meeting in the early 90s with my Higher Calling businessmen accountability group, we had two missionaries as special guests. Pastor, Bob Stevenson, and Pastor, Oralio, from Mexico attended our meeting to share what they were doing in Mexico.

That particular morning, I was depressed and struggling with the fact of how broken our family was with our daughter having major challenges, and it seemed like there was no light at the end of the tunnel. I was in a really dark place.

After pastor Stevenson and Oralio shared what they were doing in Mexico City, they asked what each of us was struggling with. I am not sure what else was shared but finally, I opened up and said our family is broken and not sure how we would get through the mess.

Everyone gathered around me and laid hands on me. They prayed over me for a long-time sharing promises from God's Word and then this verse of affirmation was shared.

Ecclesiastes 4:12

"And if one can overpower him who is alone, two can resist him. A cord of three strands is not quickly torn apart."

This verse from *Ecclesiastes 4:12* still resonates with me today as I venture out in our Sweatshirt of Hope ministry.

I will never forget that morning of promise and affirmation that God is with us and will not forsake us no matter what the situation is. We are loved by God in all situations! This Bible verse rang true today while facing challenges and was a reminder God is with us in times of despair.

As I started working full-time in the ministry, we looked at all the needs around us asking the question "How can we connect people with needs to the non-profit organizations we were working with?"

Our tagline is "Linking HOPE 4 LIFE" bringing our community together, to understand mental, physical, and spiritual needs and sharing resources for a healthier community. This needed some type of platform to connect persons with organizations.

In early 2022 we hired a woman to develop a website where people can go to find resources for life's struggles. The person can click on one of the images displayed on our website and find organizations that offer resources for the issue.

I was HUNGRY YOU gave me FOOD

I was a STRANGER and YOU WELCOMED ME

I was NEEDY and YOU SUPPORTED ME

I was NAKED and YOU CLOTHED ME

I was SICK and YOU CARED for ME

I was in PRISON and YOU CAME TO ME

Chapter 11
Journey with Purpose

My life's journey has been challenging, rocky, and dangerous for many years. I have been in some really low places mentally, dealing with depression and struggling to survive over the years. However, God had a plan I could not have imagined. God brought me from the darkest pits of hell to a life abundant in His timing to help and encourage me and others in their time of struggle.

As I grow spiritually, I realize that life is not about me, but how God wants to use me and the gifts he blessed me with for His Honor and Glory. Life is not what I did, what I achieved, how much money I made, or what title is behind my name. I am a Christ follower, and my identity is in Jesus Christ!

As I serve the Lord being content with the gifts given me, there is no greater joy than to point people to Christ in the midst of their despair. I do my best to be vulnerable and share some of my stories allowing a safe place for them to open up and share their hurts and struggles. They need to know they are not the only person traveling a challenging ride in life. It is ok not to be ok.

I do my best to share how I saw light in my darkest times and how I needed to stay focused on Jesus by reading scripture, and devotionals, listening to songs of faith, remaining connected to a local fellowship of believers, and having coffee with a trusted friend.

We are not made to walk this path alone. My daily prayer is that others will see Jesus in me and through me through my words and actions.

When the Lord leads me, I will share some scripture that may encourage others.

Isaiah 41:10

"So do not fear, for I am with you; do not be dismayed, for I am your God. I will strengthen you and help you; I will uphold you with my righteous right hand."

Psalm 28:7

"The Lord is my strength and my shield;

my heart trusts in him, and he helps me.

My heart leaps for joy, and with my song I praise him."

Psalm 51:10-12

"David prayed: Create in me a clean heart, O God, and renew a right spirit within me. Cast me not away from your presence, and take not your Holy Spirit from me. Restore to me the joy of your salvation, and uphold me with a willing spirit."

I am blessed to receive messages and testimonies of how people wearing **HOPE**-printed apparel have experienced opportunities to share the gospel because of the printed message. "HOPE God Loves You!" I personally experienced divine appointment when wearing HOPE-printed apparel. They ask what **HOPE** means which allows me to tell my story and how God continues to draw me to Him.

I am truly humbled that God would choose me, a broken person, to lead this ministry and have a passion for those struggling and the lost in our community. It is only by His grace that I have been found and been lifted up to care for the people our society would look down upon.

I can honestly say, God continues to give me peace through the challenges as I do my best to follow His call. James 1:12 says "Blessed be the man who perseveres under trial because when he has stood the test, he will receive the crown of life that God has promised to those who love him." God gives me a promise that I do not need to fear anything, even in the most difficult times.

Psalm 23:4

"Even though I walk through the darkest valley, I will fear no evil, for you are with me; your rod and your staff, they comfort me."

I am a sinner saved by grace and hang onto this promise:

1 John 1:9

"If we confess our sins, he is faithful and just and will forgive our sins."

Looking back to our early years my dream was to be a successful businessman able to support our family and follow the dreams of our culture. I always dreamed of taking extended vacations, traveling, eating out regularly, and having a vacation home without worries about finances. Could those dreams lead to an empty heart and no joy or focus? Did God say when he gave me this life "I don't need another one of those?" Did God say "be about my business?" "You are my chosen?" God calls each of us to himself in various ways for His Glory.

The question I want to pose to you is "Are you answering God's call in your life?" I will be honest, answering God's call was very difficult and not easy but I knew I had to follow His call and be faithful. Today, I can truly say God gives me peace only He can give in the midst of my journey and brokenness.

As I write this and we come to a close of 2022, a number of groups and ministries have been reaching out for sweatshirts, so they are able to take the message of **HOPE** to the streets of Philadelphia and other locations. They take food, sweatshirts, socks, and the gospel to those living on the streets, under the L, and those living in a tent city a drug-infested area of Philly. We are only able to donate **HOPE** sweatshirts to these outreach ministries based on our incoming funds so anyone interested in supporting these willing workers your financial gifts are appreciated.

God is doing amazing work so we **PRAISE HIM** giving all Glory to God…

I want to Thank God for allowing my wife and I to weather the storms of life together for 54 years of marriage as of 2022. We have been truly blessed! A large percentage of marriages end in divorce when there is someone struggling with addiction in the family. Thank You Jesus for your grace and mercy on us!

When we have Jesus in our life "All is Well."

I want to share one key factor that helped me through many difficult days and that was my daily prayer walk. I started my daily prayer walks back in 1983 when I was having major health issues due to a lot of stress from being in a business partnership. I was hospitalized for a week, not caring if I lived or died. I was depressed and walked away from my business partnership and didn't work for 3 months. I went on walks four to five times a day crying out to God in pain, anger, frustration, and many times not sure what I felt.

After my wife and I started another business, I continued to take some walks, but not daily until 1994 when the economy tanked and our business came to a crashing halt. We had to lay off 55 employees at that point, and I made a commitment to start walking every day early in the morning before sunrise. I have been taking my daily prayer walks since 1994 and still continue walking early each morning. This is a special time for me, my quiet time with, no phone, and no earbuds, and a time to focus on creation and God's many blessings. A time to cry out to God for help in the midst of darkness and prayer requests. I treasure this special time more and more each day.

Chapter 12
Unity

As I come to the closing chapter of this book and a long journey, my prayer is there may be unity in our family, in the church, and with all God's people.

If today is my last day on earth our prayer is that our son and daughter have reconciled, forgiven each other, love each other, and serve our God in the name of Jesus for His honor and His glory!

Ephesians 1:7-10

"In him we have redemption through his blood, the forgiveness of sins, in accordance with the riches of God's grace [8] that he lavished on us. With all wisdom and understanding, he made known to us the mystery of his will according to his good pleasure, which he purposed in Christ, to be put into effect when the times reach their fulfillment—to bring unity to all things in heaven and on earth under Christ."

I want each of our family, son, daughter, granddaughters, great-granddaughters, and adopted family to know that they are loved by my wife and me. We love each of you for who you are, and for your God-given gifts and abilities. Each of you is special, created by God, and in the image of God. You are valued for who you are no matter what road of life you choose.

Romans 3:23.

"We have all sinned and fallen short of the glory of God."

I plead for forgiveness for the many times I messed up and for not always addressing the issues at hand, but want each of you to know I did the best at the time. I ask for forgiveness for working long hours as I did my best to provide for and meet the needs of our family.

Our prayer for each of you is that you have totally surrendered your life to Christ, laid all your burdens at the foot of the cross, and are serving God in some capacity.

We love our son and daughter in the midst of turmoil and did not disown or abandon either of you no matter what you did or what was said because Jesus did not disown me when I sin. Jesus loved me and went to the cross for my sins and died a brutal death for me so I may have life eternal.

We had to learn very hard lessons not to enable those who choose a path of destruction but always loved and did our best to give grace in the midst of tough love.

Ephesians 1:6

"to the praise of his glorious grace, which he has freely given us in the One he loves."

We pray our granddaughters are able to forgive their mom for begin absent from their lives for many years and that God will restore everything that has been lost.

Luke 15:4

"Suppose one of you has a hundred sheep and loses one of them. Doesn't he leave the ninety-nine in the open country and go after the **lost** sheep until he finds it?"

Luke 15:6

"and goes home. Then he calls his friends and neighbors together and says, 'Rejoice with me; I have found my lost sheep.'"

Luke 15:32

"But we had to celebrate and be glad because this brother of yours was dead and is alive again; he was lost and is found."

To each of our family: God loves each of you and never gives up loving you, so let us not give up loving each other in Jesus' Name, Amen.

As we bring our journey to a close my prayer is our story was educational, informative, and encouraging, and will motivate anyone struggling to seek help and support. Do not hide in the darkness of your struggles due to shame, guilt, and failure. The reason for writing this book is to encourage you to keep looking up in the darkest times of your life because Jesus is preparing a mountaintop experience. Jesus does shine in the darkness if we do not allow Satan to poison our minds. So, keep looking up my friend!

For additional information go to SweathshirtofHope.org.

My e-mail address is Terry@SweatshirtofHope.org

Review

" The stories we tell are never just our own. In 'Helpless and Hopeless,' Terry Derstine reveals a story of tragedy and overcoming, of suffering and faith that speak for many suffering in silence. A message of hope, his experiences resonate with those whose individual versions vary only in the details. Many of us share the pain, the regrets, the shame and even guilt of private losses; we endure unspeakable trials. Yet we are embraced by the love of Jesus Christ and do not need to bear our burdens alone. Derstine reminds us that helpless never means hopeless."

C.D. Baker, author of '101 Cups of Water'.

Review

"The horrific backstory and Terry Derstine's writings provide us with the clear purpose and mission of Sweatshirt of Hope. As we read the account most of us naturally will cry out to God and ask WHY! It's easy for us to refer to a couple of familiar Bible verses as Terry mentions, but let's try to walk in his shoes as we read the story. All of a sudden, we may realize, could this be the very reason the wonderful ministry of Sweatshirt of Hope exists? While the darkness for Terry and Linda is still very real and unresolved the bright light of Sweatshirt of Hope moves forward." A good read for all.

Clare Moyer, retired business owner, Life Trek Assn., founder

Review

"From helpless and hopeless to Hopeful and eventually to Hope Filled! That's what you will find in this real-life struggle of parenting a child and now adult, gripped with addiction. I thought I knew the journey of Terry and his wife Linda, I did not. This book is filled with raw emotion and real Hope for those struggling with addiction and for those who care and love them!"

- John Yoast

Review

"NO STIGMA! NO SHAME! Terry's poignant story details the heart-breaking impact of his daughter's addiction on him and his family. Recognizing that his story is not unique, Terry reminds us that addiction does not discriminate. We all know someone who is struggling, someone in recovery, or someone who has died from drug use/overdose. His story is a call for us all to work together to break the cycle, reduce stigma, and spread hope."

-Ryan Schweiger - Certified Recovery Specialist

Made in the USA
Middletown, DE
06 November 2023